BRUNO & FRIDA
Go To Mexico City
Written by Gary Mallon
Illustrated by Melissa Vandiver

For Elsa Maria Cristina Tesara, a beloved
mother, wife, and grandmother

"I have always dreamed of visiting Mexico City!" says Patrick, grinning with delight.

"The world-famous artist Frida Kahlo was born here, and I know how much you love her," says José. "You even named our Frida after her!"

Patrick nods. "I definitely want to see her paintings while we're here. Let's go!" "See ya, Bruno! Adios, Frida!" says Jose, giving them each a loving pat on the head. "Stay out of trouble, please!"

"Mexico City is so big and there is so much to see," says Patrick. "It's a good thing we have this map." He puts it in his pocket.

But as they head out the door, the map falls out of Patrick's pocket but he doesn't realize it.

Frida slumps on the floor and gives a low growl. She never likes being left behind. Bruno is secretly relieved to be staying in the hotel room. He feels at home wherever he is, and now he happily rolls onto his back with his legs in the air and enjoys the sunshine streaming in through the window.

"I would really love to see the house where Frida Kahlo lived," grumbles Frida. "Why didn't Jose and Patrick bring me along? Of course, I could take myself there, but I don't know where it is."

"You could always use the map," Bruno suggests lazily. "Patrick accidentally dropped it by the door. And I was watching when he circled the street where the other Frida used to live. Her house is called Casa Azul and it's not far at all. Even I could walk there."

Frida looks at her brother in amazement and exclaims, "Bruno! I'm so proud of you! You're usually not so brave!"

"Well, I'm not saying we should do it," Bruno starts to say, but Frida is already running in excited circles around the room and thinking out loud: "After Casa Azul, we'll explore the rest of Mexico City!"

Bruno has a sinking feeling. "Oh no! What have I done? I'm already sorry I mentioned that map."

But there is no stopping Frida once she has an adventure in mind, so off they go, slipping out of the hotel unnoticed and then racing down the sidewalk toward Coyoacán, the neighborhood where the famous artist Frida Kahlo once lived with her family.

When they arrive at the Casa Azul, Bruno is panting and ready to lie down in the shade and rest. But Frida has more energy than ever. To their disappointment, the large green front door is locked. They stand on their hind legs and peek through the window. They see a glowing light inside and someone moving.

"Bruno, doesn't that look like a person walking back and forth as if they were waiting for visitors?" asks Frida.

Bruno squints at the figure. "It looks like a ghost!" The fur on his back stands up. Bruno is afraid of ghosts. Frida, on the other hand, has always thought it would be fascinating to meet a ghost.

She spots a ladder on the side of the
house. "Let's climb up to get over the wall," she
says. "It's an easy climb and we can get in over that wall." She
doesn't wait for an answer, but runs to the ladder and starts climbing.

Bruno follows reluctantly. He whimpers to himself, "I don't like
ladders. I don't like sneaking into places. And I don't like ghosts!"

As he makes his way up the ladder, Bruno is so anxious that he sneezes so hard it shakes the ladder. He and Frida both give a yelp as they lose their balance and start to tumble through the air inside the walls of the Casa Azul.

But suddenly strong arms reach out to catch them both and gently settle them on the ground.

They turn to see who saved them and find a beautiful, dark-haired woman with colorful flowers in her hair. She is dressed in a traditional Mexican dress draped with a red, fringed shawl.

"Hola, my friends, I am Frida Kahlo. This is not the way most people come into my home, but welcome to Casa Azul."

"I knew we would find you, Frida!" says Frida the Frenchie. Bruno is white-faced with fear. She has to be a ghost!

"Bruno, let me explain" she says. "Today is the second day of November, which is a day when people in Mexico celebrate the Día de los Muertos. That means the Day of the Dead"

"Dia de los Muertos? That sounds scary," says Bruno nervously.

"Don't be afraid of the Dia de los Muertos," says Frida Kahlo with a reassuring smile. "It is a festive holiday. In our tradition, on this day the souls of our loved ones who have passed away are able to return home for a visit. That is why I'm home today. And I'm so glad I was, because you seemed to need my help."

"Thank you for helping us, Frida!" says Frida the Frenchie. "I have always been a big fan of yours. We're sorry that we tried to get inside your house without permission, but we heard how beautiful it is and we wanted to see it."

"As much as it would be my pleasure to show you my beloved house, where I lived with my family and my husband, Diego Rivera, we don't want to miss the celebration in the Zócalo Plaza. You will love it, I promise."

Bruno finds that he is surprisingly comfortable chatting with a spirit. He laughs to himself as he thinks "Wow, this Frida is as bossy as my sister! I like her."

"Is it far?" asks Bruno. "I'm a little tired..."

Frida Kahlo winks at him and looks at her feet. "Feet, what do I need you for when I have wings to fly?" And suddenly the two pups and the famous artist are whisked away to the Zócalo Plaza, carried on a magical wind.

When they arrive at the Plaza, Bruno's relief quickly turns to alarm. It is crowded with skeletons! But he takes a closer look and realizes they are just people with painted faces, wearing costumes.

Frida the Frenchie has read about this. "They dress as skeletons to remember their loved ones who have passed on, and to celebrate the cycle of life. Nothing to be afraid of, Bruno."

"You are such a smart girl," says Frida Kahlo. "No wonder they named you after me. Since you are little Frida, I am renaming you Fridita." Fridita prances around importantly and the artist Frida laughs at her antics.

Bruno rolls his eyes. Frida is showing off again. Secretly, he's a little jealous. Why doesn't he get a nickname?

"Hey, I have an idea," says Frida Kahlo, "let's get you both costumes for the festivities. There is a very stylish skeleton who wears fancy clothes and an elegant floppy hat. We call her La Catrina. Let's dress you like her, my little Fridita."

Fridita loves her new costume and even sits still so the artist can paint her face. When Fridita's transformation into La Catrina is almost complete, Bruno starts to say,

"Fridita, you look like a ..."

But before he can finish his
thought, a skeleton band marches
by and one of the band members
grabs Bruno by his paw. As if he is
as light as a feather. Bruno sails
up into the air and disappears
into the crowd.

"Oh, no! If I lose Bruno I will be in so much trouble," cries Fridita.

"Don't worry, my sweet namesake, I know those guys. Bruno will be fine with them, and I'll help you find him" says Frida Kahlo.

"Do you see those colorful altars over there? Those are called ofrendas. Families assemble them to remember their loved ones. We decorate them with marigold flowers, pictures of those who have passed away, and many of the foods they enjoyed in life---to nourish their spirit. We also place sugar skulls called calaveras de azúcar, and papel picado, which are colorful paper flags with picture cutouts for decoration."

Fridita is enjoying learning about Día de los Muertos and watching the people walk by in colorful costumes. She almost forgets to worry where Bruno is. But then she catches sight of José and Patrick in the Plaza looking at the ofrendas. "If they find out we snuck out and I've lost Bruno, I'll be in big trouble" she thinks, hoping they won't recognize her in her Catrina costume.

Suddenly, a skeleton band marches by. Frida Kahlo laughs and points to the smallest band member. "Doesn't he look familiar to you?" she asks Fridita.

Looking more closely, Fridita realizes it's Bruno wearing bells around his neck and dressed as a skeleton too!

"Bruno!" calls Fridita, but the music is too loud. He is happily marching along as Fridita and Frida run to catch up. When the song ends Bruno hears his sister call his name and gives a happy bark. He thanks his fellow band members for all the fun and joins the two Fridas.

"I told you not to worry," says Frida Kahlo "Welcome back, Bruno. You seem to have some musical talent."

"They asked me to cover for one of their missing band members," says Bruno, puffing out his chest with pride. "Mariachi music is so joyful. We danced, we sang, and we celebrated."

"Brother, you had me so worried, but I'm glad you're back," exclaims Fridita.

To celebrate Bruno's return, Frida Kalho treats them to snacks at a café, They try some traditional Dia de los Muertos food. There are tacos, tamales, a special bread called pan de muerto, and a sweet, milky drink called horchata.

Fridita gulps down her taco and notices that Frida is not eating anything.

Frida Kahlo explains, "Mija, as a spirit we don't eat in the traditional way. We are nourished by absorbing the aromas and energy of the food."

"Then you never have to brush your teeth," says Bruno, who hates to have his teeth brushed.

Frida Kahlo laughs. "You are both delightful! But my time with you is running short, my dear friends. I am only here for one evening, so I need to get you both back to the Casa Azul."

And just like that, they are whisked away on a magical wind back to Frida Kalho's house. But this time, they are inside the house. Fridita looks around eagerly.

"I brought you to my studio to show you something special," says Frida Kahlo. At the wave of her hand, brushes and multicolored paints swirl in the air, they mix together and burst onto a blank canvas sitting on an easel in the corner. Before their eyes, the artist creates an enchanting new painting.

As Bruno and Fridita watch with amazement, they both realize something at the same time.

"That's us!" they cry.

"I have loved my beautiful animal friends all my life, and since you two have been so special to me tonight I wanted to put you in my painting. It is my gift to you," says Frida Kahlo.

Under the stars and twinkling lights outside Frida's studio, a path of marigold flowers appears. It is time for the spirits to follow it home. Frida Kahlo hugs Bruno and Fridita. She twirls in a circle, taking a last look at her beloved home, and then moves toward the light and the swirl of copal incense. Fridita thinks she must be floating. The artist turns and blow them a kiss.

"Remember my friends, and especially you my beautiful little namesake: Viva la Vida! Long live life! Celebrate life and enjoy it to the fullest!" And with that she vanishes into a million sparking lights.

"Wow! What an incredible exit," said Fridita while Bruno's mouth just hangs open.

Fridita has an idea, "Let's leave our painting here at the Casa Azul. Millions of people visit Frida's home, and they will be able to appreciate it! It will be fun for our painting to live here at the Casa Azul."

 "We'll be famous!" says Bruno.

"Bruno, it's time for us to get back to our hotel. We don't want Patrick and José to realize we snuck out," says Fridita.

Using their four paws, running at full speed, they noticed as they ran that their makeup and costumes started to disappear at if the magic wore off. They ran so fast that they made it back to their hotel in record time.

Bruno, who hates to be out of breath, thinks to himself that he liked it better when Frida Kahlo used her magic wind.

Minutes later, Patrick and José return. "We're home!" they announce, giving Bruno and Frida belly rubs. "Were you bored?" asks José.

"I wish we could have taken you," says Patrick. "We saw so many beautiful paintings by Frida Kahlo and we even saw a Mariachi skeleton band. One of the members looked just like you, Bruno!"

As they cuddle together in their bed later that night, Bruno whispers, "Sweet dreams, sister.- I know I never want to go, but I do love our adventures together."

"Sleep tight, brother. You were so brave tonight," says Fridita.

Suddenly, they both hear a faint voice whispering from above. "Good night, my little ones. Viva la Vida!"

www.ingramcontent.com/pod-product-compliance
Lightning Source LLC
Chambersburg PA
CBRC101624100726
47973CB00022B/258